The Urbana Free Library

To renew: call 217-367-4057
or go to *urbanafreelibrary.org*
and select "My Account"

Meet Milo at the Mall

• Respecting Property •

By T. M. Merk

Published by The Child's World®
1980 Lookout Drive • Mankato, MN 56003-1705
800-599-READ • www.childsworld.com

Photographs: Monkey Business Images/Shutterstock.com,
cover, 1, 7, 19; Aleoks/Shutterstock.com, 5; dasytnik/
Shutterstock.com, 9; Tyler Olson/Shutterstock.com, 11;
Iakov Filimonov/Shutterstock.com, 13; wavebreakmedia/
Shutterstock.com, 15; Photographee.eu/Shutterstock.com, 17
Icons: © Aridha Prassetya/Dreamstime, 3, 5, 7, 8, 11, 12, 14, 22

ISBN HARDCOVER: 9781503827479
ISBN PAPERBACK: 9781622434428
LCCN: 2017961937

Printed in the United States of America
PA02379

About the Author

T.M. Merk is an elementary educator
with a master's degree in elementary
education from Lesley University in
Cambridge, Massachusetts. Drawing
on years of classroom experience, she
enjoys creating engaging educational
material that inspires students' passion
for learning. She lives in New Hampshire
with her husband and her dog, Finn.

Table of Contents

Milo wanted a new paint set. His parents took him to the mall to buy one. Leo the paintbrush helped him pick it out.

Your **property** is anything that belongs to you. It can be something you bought, something another person gave you, or even something you made!

"That's a neat paint set! Can I use it when we get home?" Milo's little sister asked.

"Yes," Milo said. "But please don't wreck it."

Other people might ask to use your property. Then you have to decide if you want to share. If someone tries to use your property without asking you, that is **disrespectful**.

Just then, Milo saw **graffiti** painted on a wall inside the store.

"Why did someone paint on the wall?" he wondered.

Graffiti is writing or drawings on a public surface that have been put there without **permission**. If you think you should write or draw on something that is not your property, you should always ask first. If the owner of the property says no, you need to respect his or her answer.

"That's a good question," Leo said from inside Milo's bag. He peeked out. "It's time to brush up on respect. Painting on the wall like that is **discourteous** to the owner of the store."

"It's just paint," Milo said. "Is it really a big deal?"

Store owners work hard to keep their stores neat and organized for shoppers. If people put graffiti on a store wall, the store owner might have to spend money to clean it off. Although painting can be a lot of fun, a wall is not the right place to paint, unless you have the owner's permission.

"Yes!" Leo said. "Property is something that is owned by a person or business. If it's not yours, you should not paint on it, break it, or change it at all."

Many stores have warning signs when their goods are **fragile**, which means breakable. Often, if you break something in a store, you have to pay for it. If you do not plan to buy something, it is respectful to not touch it, even if it looks like it is really cool! "Hands off" is always the best policy!

13

"That makes me think of the books in my classroom," Milo said. "My teacher taught us to **respect** them. We shouldn't write on them or rip out their pages. They are for everyone, even next year's class!"

All classroom materials should be treated with respect. Classroom supplies like electronics, headphones, markers, and crayons are breakable and should be handled with care. These items are for everyone to use and can be expensive to replace.

"That's right," Leo said. "You can respect property in other ways, too. If you borrow something from another person, you should be careful with it and return it when you promised."

"I want my sister to be careful with my paint set," Milo said. "That means I want her to respect my property!"

Leo nodded. "We should always respect books, buildings, and other people's things."

Respectful Talk

Do you need help talking in a respectful way about your property or other people's property? Use these sentence starters to help!

- I'm using this right now, but ...

- This is my _____, but I will share it with you. Please be careful.

- Please keep my _____ clean and unbroken if you use it and return it to where it belongs when you are done.

- _____ is for everyone to use. Please share.

- _____ is not for everyone to use. Please do not touch it.

- May I please borrow your _____? I promise to treat it respectfully and give it back.

S.T.E.A.M. Activity

Design a Protective Case

Directions: Using any materials that you choose, design a case that will protect a piece of property. If the property belongs to someone else, be sure to ask before you take it. The case should keep the property from being scratched or broken.

Time Constraints: You may use a total of 30 minutes to complete this project. You are allowed 10 minutes to plan and 20 minutes to build the case. When you're done, store the property in your case for safe keeping!

Discussion: Did you take time to think about what would be the safest way to store the property? Were you very careful when you touched it? How did you feel when you were done? What worked really well? What could you do better next time?

Suggested Materials:

- Shoebox
- Cardboard rolls
- Cotton balls
- Pipe cleaners
- Popsicle sticks
- Plastic wrap
- Tape/glue
- Safety scissors
- Markers/crayons

Glossary

discourteous: (diss-KUR-tee-us) When someone is discourteous, he or she is impolite or rude.

disrespectful: (diss-rih-SPEKT-full) When someone is disrespectful, that person does not show that he or she cares about other people, places, things, or ideas.

fragile: (FRA-jul) Something is fragile if it is easily damaged or is breakable.

graffiti: (gruh-FEE-tee) Graffiti is writing or drawings on a public surface that have been put there without permission.

permission: (per-MIH-shun) Permission is being allowed to do something or go somewhere.

property: (PRAH-per-tee) Property is something that is owned by a person or business.

respect: (rih-SPEKT) To respect is to show that you care about a person, place, thing, or idea.

To Learn More

Books

Cook, Julia. *Ricky Sticky Fingers.* Chattanooga, TN: National Center for Youth Issues, 2012.

Meiners, Cheri J. *Respect and Take Care of Things (Learning to Get Along).* Minneapolis, MN: Free Spirit Publishing, 2004.

Moses, Brian. *"I Don't Care!" Learning About Respect.* London, UK: Wayland (Publishers) Ltd., 1998.

Web Sites

Visit our Web site for links about respecting property:
childsworld.com/links

Note to Parents, Teachers, and Librarians: We routinely verify our Web links to make sure they are safe and active sites. So encourage your readers to check them out!

Index